About the author

Once described in *The Times* in London as the *'Delia Smith of Korean Cooking'*, Seoul born Yongja Kim moved to America in her early 20's. Yongja's career since that time has included her own tv shows in New York and as a guest on Korean radio.

A cooking instructor since 1993, Yongja also contributed as a columnist to the New York edition of the prestigious *Korea Times* for over 25 years. She is the author of a previously acclaimed book of cookery and frequently demonstrated the art of Korean cuisine to diplomatic groups visiting America.

Having co-judged an important global event dedicated to Korean cuisine, Yongja later contributed to the book *'Rags to Riches'*, dedicated to the incredible economic rise of South Korea from its time of poverty and war. She was one of 60 international personalities featured in the official publication of the G20 conference of world leaders in Seoul.

Yongja now lives in London, England with her husband, retired music magazine editor and publisher Alan Smith.

Yongja Kim's Easy Guide to Korean Cooking is an updated and revised version of her English language book Korean Cuisine (2009-out of print).

Other publications: 1995 *Food of The West* (cookbook) in Korean
2009 *Korean Cuisine* (cookbook) in English
2010 *A Feast for You* (travel & food stories) in Korean

About the photographer

My thanks to US based food writer and photographer Erin Gleeson who provided most of the photographs in this book. Erin has been published by *Gourmet* magazine, the *New York Times* and is the author of several cookbooks of her own.

Yongja Kim
PUBLISHING

Text, Recipes & Design Copyright © 2021 Yongja Kim
All rights reserved.
Photography Erin Gleeson
Design, creative and production - www.spiffingcovers.com

Published by Yongja Kim Publishing 2021
Paperback ISBN 978-1-7399187-0-5
Hardback ISBN 978-1-7399187-2-9
eBook ISBN - 978-1-7399187-1-2

For Clayton, Sienna and Charlotte

Welcome to My World of Korean Cooking

If you love Korean food or would just like to try something new, I hope you'll love my new book *Yongja Kim's Easy Guide to Korean Cooking*.

In these pages I celebrate, update or rediscover the very best of my home country's delicious favourite dishes. My childhood memories certainly live again as I recall the aromas in the kitchen of my grandmother's house. Wide-eyed, I used to watch with affection as she prepared wonderful combination dishes of traditional country food and and fine cuisine.

You'll find a handy list in the book of essential ingredients and spices and advice on where to find them. I suggest you set them aside in your own special 'Korean Store Cupboard'. Hopefully *Bibimbap, Bulgogi, Cholpan Gui* and *Japche* may soon become familiar favourites!

Don't worry if you're not a natural when cooking Korean or any other food. I confess: neither was I! I can be clumsy, although I do always take comfort in my two important words: Creativity and Concentration.

It's a cliché, but true: practice really does make perfect.
After this, as we say in Korea, *Masikkeh deseyo!* *

Yongja

*Enjoy your meal!

Contents

MEAT & SEAFOOD

Hot! Hot! Chilli Mackerel with Potato and Onion *(Godung-o Jorim)* 12
Sizzling Barbecue Beef *(Bulgogi)* 14
Hot & Sweet Pork Belly *(Samgyopsal Gui)* 16
Grilled Jumbo Shrimp *(Daeha Jijim)* 18
Spring Onion Salad *(Pahmuchim)* 19
Hearty Braised Short Ribs *(Galbi Chim)* 20
Jidan (The Traditional Garnish) 23
Golden Peppered Chicken with Onion *(Dak Chim)* 24
Braised Sea Bass with Chunky Radish *(Sengsun Chim)* 26
Tabletop-grilled Steak & Veg with Tofu *(Cholpan Gui)* 28
Spicy Grilled Pollock *(Bugo Gui)* 30

ONE DISH MEALS

Rub for Flavour Pork Bibimbap 34
Other Suggestions for Bibimbap 36
Cool Summer Shrimp Noodles *(Bibim Guksu)* 38
Another Combination for a Cold Noodle Dish 40

TOFU & MORE *(Banchan – Warm Side Dishes)*

Ginger & Lemon Crispy Tofu *(Dubu Jijim)* 44
Silken Seasoned Tofu *(Yangnyom Dubu)* 1 46
Seasoned Tofu with Pollock Roe *(Yangnyom Dubu)* 2 48
Tasty Grilled Tofu *(Dubu Jorim)* 50
Lemon Grilled Scallops on a Stick *(Kwanja Gui)* 52
Skewered Beef with Mushrooms & Carrots *(Sanjok)* 54
Bean Pancake with Seafood & Bacon *(Bindaettok)* 56
Beef & Vegetables with Clear Noodles *(Japche)* 58
Why We Celebrate *Chuseok* - The Full Moon Festival 60

VEGETARIAN SIDES & KIMCHI *(Banchan)*

Steamed Courgette with Seasoned Soy *(Hobak Chim)* 64
Spicy Asparagus *(Asparagus Muchim)* 66
Sweet & Sour Radish Salad *(Musengche)* 68
Refreshing Seaweed Salad *(Miyok Muchim)* 70
Lemon Spinach with Pepper *(Sigumchi Namul)* 72
Crunchy Bean Sprouts *(Sukju Namul)* 74
Nutty Soya Bean Sprouts *(Kong Namul)* 76

Green Chilli Potato Strips *(Gamja Bokum)* 78
Chrysanthemum Green Salad *(Ssukat Muchim)* 80
Chilli Cucumber *(Oee Namul)* 82
Chilli Cabbage (Kimchi) 84
White *Kimchi (Baek Kimchi)* 88
The *Kimchi* story 90

MY GRANDMA, MY INSPIRATION
.... 92

PREPARING RICE FAST & SLOW
Fast Rice 96
Slower But Tastier 97

SOUPS & PORRIDGE
Birthday Soup *(Miyok Guk)* 100
New Year's Day Beef Soup *(Ttokguk)* 102
Beef Bone Broth 104
Our Festive Dish for A Special Occasions 105
Tofu Stew With Beef Bone Broth *(Dubu Chigae)* 106
Spinach Clam Soup *(Jogae Sigumchi Guk)* 108
Kelp Broth *(Dashima Gukmul)* 109
Cold Seaweed Soup with Cucumber *(Miyok Nengguk)* 110
Porridge with Pine Nuts *(Jaatjuk)* 112

DESSERTS
Honey Persimmon & Lime *(Dan Gaam)* 116
Summer Watermelon Smoothie *(Whache)* 118
Baked Sweet Sweet Potato *(Goon Goguma)* 120
Tangy Orange with Fruit Preserve *(Yujachong Orange)* 122
Chestnuts with Dates and Sweet Rice *(Yaksik)* 124
Red Bean Purée with Sweet Rice Balls *(Patjuk)* 126

AND FINALLY...
How It All Began 128
Your Must-Have Korean Store Cupboard 130
Your Where To Buy A-Z 132
Thank You! 134

Meat
AND
Seafood

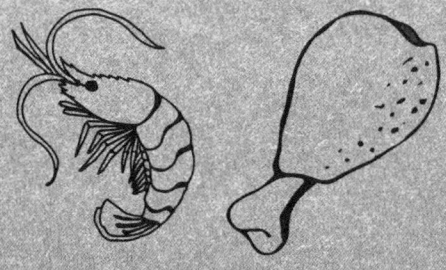

Choose 2 or 3 mild
side dishes for a spicy
main course or the
other way around.
Always balance mild
and spicy food.

Hot! Hot! Chilli Mackerel with Potatoes and Onion

(GODUNG-O CHIM)

Mackerel is an oily high protein fish which is great for heart health. However for this dish I have added the extra kick of chilli, onions, garlic and ginger.

Ask your friendly fishmonger to fillet the fish on one side, leaving the bone attached on the other before cutting it into chunks. Don't go home without the head or bones as they give the broth a wonderful depth of flavour.

This dish has often been made with an Asian variety of radish, but for my recipe I would like you to try the comforting taste of Charlotte potatoes. American readers should try Yukon Gold.

Ingredients

SERVES 4

600g/1.3lbs 2 MACKEREL, cut chunks
1 tbsp CHILLI PASTE *(gochujang)*
3 cups WATER
2 tbsp CHILLI FLAKES (coarse *gochugaru*)
2 tbsp SOY SAUCE

1 medium ONION
VEGETABLE OIL
2 GARLIC CLOVES, crushed
250g POTATOES, sliced 1.3 cm/ ½" thick
3 SPRING ONIONS, cut large chunks
1 thumb size GINGER in strips

Method

1. Put the chilli paste in a sieve over a bowl with 3 cups of water. Press the paste with the back of a spoon until dissolved through to the water. Add chilli flakes and soy sauce. Set aside.

2. Start cooking by stir-frying the onions with oil until translucent, then add two garlic cloves.
Spread the onions and garlic evenly in the pan. Place potato pieces and then the mackerel on top. Pour over the chilli soya spiced water.

3. Cover and cook for approximately 20-25 minutes basting frequently until the potatoes are soft. Add ginger, spring onions and cook for 3 minutes more. If you still have lots of liquid, open the cover and baste the ingredients until the liquid has reduced to half.

Sizzling Barbecue Beef

(BULGOGI)

I love this delicious treat for four or more, direct from the grill. Use ribeye or sirloin cut in thin slices. Your butcher may do this for you.

Ingredients

SERVES 4

680g/ 1 ½ lbs BEEF RIBEYE or SIRLOIN, sliced 3-4mm (1/8") thick

MARINADE:

4 tbsp SOY SAUCE
2 tbsp WATER
1 ½ tbsp SESAME OIL

4 tsp golden caster SUGAR
2 tsp toasted SESAME SEEDS
2 GARLIC CLOVES, crushed fine
2 SPRING ONIONS, chopped
1 SPRING ONION, cut for garnish
¼ cored, peeled and grated Asian PEAR (optional)

Method

1. Prepare the marinade and drizzle over the sliced meat. If your grill has wide ridges, lightly place a large sheet of aluminium foil over them. Make plenty of holes to allow heat circulation. Grill over moderate heat until the meat turns opaque. Turn over and cook until lightly browned. Serve hot.

For a cold lunch variation in the summer cook the ribeye or sirloin steak (normal steak thickness) at medium, then cool. Slice thin and drizzle the marinade.

Hot & Sweet Pork Belly

(SAMGYUPSAL GUI)

The Korean name of this dish, *Samgyupsal*, means three layer meat and refers to the look of the pork belly skin, fat and flesh.

It's a fatty dish... However Korean food is generally so lean that occasionally you may like it as a tasty special treat.

Personally I prefer this more than barbecued beef! Try also with a lettuce wrap *(Ssam)*.

Ingredients

SERVES 4

568g /1 ¼ lbs PORK BELLY, sliced 6mm (1/4")

1 SPRING ONION, cut diagonally for garnish

Hot & Sweet MARINADE:

4 tbsp CHILLI PASTE *(gochujang)*

2 tsp CHILLI FLAKES *(coarse gochugaru)*
2 tbsp SUGAR
1 tbsp grated GINGER
4 tsp SOY SAUCE
2 GARLIC CLOVES, crushed

Method

1. When using an open grill outdoors, first brush or spoon over just half of the prepared sauce.
If using the oven, keep the meat 10cm (4") away from the grill (heat source). Use a ridged pan so the fat can drip away; otherwise the meat sits in its own fat and reduces its lovely crispiness. It should be ready in 5 or so minutes; after this turn the meat and brush or spoon over with the rest of the sauce.

2. Then cook for 3 minutes more or until lightly browned. To serve, cut bite-size with scissors.

Grilled Jumbo Shrimp

(DAEHA JIJIM)

Shelled or unshelled, this dish makes a beautiful summer- style presentation at any time of the year. Serve on a bed of spring onion salad lightly tossed with the sauce. Try other greens like water cress if spring onion isn't to your taste.

Ingredients

SERVES 4

12 JUMBO SHRIMPS
  (600g/1.35 lbs)
VEGETABLE OIL

SAUCE:

4 tbsp SOY SAUCE

2 tbsp WATER
2 tbsp SESAME OIL
1 tbsp GRATED GINGER
2 tsp CHILLI FLAKES
  (coarse *gochugaru*)
1 tsp SUGAR

2 SPRING ONIONS or
  handful of rough cut
  chives
2 GARLIC CLOVE,
  crushed fine
1/3 LEMON for a squeeze

1. Wash the shrimps under cold running water.
Remove body shells except for the tail and one segment just below the head. This helps retain the head if required. Now make a light cut in the back of the shrimp to carefully remove the dark vein.

2. Grill the shrimps in 2 spoonfuls of oil in a non stick frying pan at medium heat. Cook both sides until pink. Add the sauce, letting the shrimps sizzle until the sauce is reduced by half. Be careful not to let it burn in the pan!
Add a squeeze of the lemon to serve.

Spring Onion Salad

(PAHMUCHIM)

With its extra kick of chilli flakes and lemon, this refreshing salad makes a great accompaniment to the Grilled Jumbo Shrimp.

Ingredients

SERVES 4

2 bunches SPRING ONION, cut
  7.5cm/3"long
2 tsp SESAME OIL

1 tsp CHILLI FLAKES (coarse *gochugaru*)
DASH of LEMON
SALT

Method

1. Cut the lengths of spring onion in fine strips and immerse in iced water with cubes for 10 minutes. Plunge the strips in and out of the water 2 or 3 times to make them curl and take away any sharp flavour. Drain well. If not serving immediately, refrigerate until needed.

2. Just before serving, add chilli flakes, sesame oil, lemon juice and a sprinkle of salt.

Hearty Braised Short Ribs with Mushrooms

(GALBI CHIM)

Although this wonderfully filling warm food may well remind you of the hearty winter beef stews popular in the West. In Korea we also love it for special occasions. In autumn — if you add in-season chestnuts and gingko nuts—it's even better!

For this dish, you'll need your loving attention and cooking and preparation for many hours. But it's a satisfying and warming experience if you have the patience.

If you do not have Asian radish, use potatoes. Cut and cook with carrots. Small new potatoes can be left whole.

Ingredients

SERVES 4

1.4 kg/3 lbs BEEF SHORT RIBS
 with bones
1 ONION, cut chunks
1 LEEK, cut half
4 GARLIC CLOVES
250g/9oz RADISH or
 Potatoes, cut chunks
4 dried SHIITAKE mushrooms,
 soaked in water until soft,
 cut chunks
2 large CARROTS, cut chunks

6 fresh CHESTNUTS (optional), peeled
10 fresh GINKGO NUTS (optional),
 shelled, inner skin peeled
3 SPRING ONIONS, cut roughly
JIDAN (page 23) for garnish

MARINADE:

½ cup SOY SAUCE
2 tbsp golden CASTER SUGAR
1 tbsp grated GINGER
1/3 KOREAN PEAR (optional), grated ▶

20

Method

COOK IN THE OVEN, finish on the hob.
I use an oven proof, 28cm/11" non stick pot.

1. Soak the dry mushrooms with water then set aside for later use.

2. Preheat the oven for 163C/325F; heat the pot until very hot; add vegetable oil and let the meat sizzle to brown on all sides. Transfer to a bowl. Lower the heat. Now stir-fry the onions until translucent and add leek, garlic and celery. Cook until the onion pieces are lightly brown here and there. Browning will add a yummy sweetness.

3. Make room in the centre of the pot for the meat. Add marinade and 5 ½ cups of water (including the mushroom liquid), to cover 2/3 of the meat. When boiling starts, transfer the pot to the heated oven and cook for 1 ¾ hours. Do not open! Turn off the oven and allow the pot and its contents to rest for another 30 minutes.

4. If you would like to make this meal extra special, make *Jidan* (page 23) while the meat is cooking and set aside.

5. Transfer the short ribs to a bowl and cover. Remove the leek and celery and set them aside. You may like to use them for flavouring for some other dish at some other time.

Transfer the liquid from the pot to a narrow container. All the fat will be on top and it will be easier to remove most of it with a spoon.

6. Cooking now transfers to the hob where you add radish and mushrooms to the pot. Pour the liquid and bring it to the boil covered. After 15-20 minutes, add carrots and chestnuts. If you still have lots of liquid, cook without the cover until the vegetables are tender and the sauce is reduced to half (about 30 minutes). Add the meat and combine well together.

As cooking continues, baste the short ribs several times. Add spring onion and ginkgo nuts and cook 2-3 minutes more. Ginkgo nuts are most delicious when chewy. Add *Jidan* for garnish if preferred. Serve with rice and spiced veg.

Jidan

(THE TRADITIONAL GARNISH FOR BRAISED SHORT RIBS)

A nice decorative topping for the braised beef short ribs (above), these simple pastry shapes are simplicity itself.

However these days Koreans use them mainly for special occasions.

Ingredients

SERVES 4

2 EGGS
1/3 tsp CORN STARCH for egg whites
½ tsp WATER for egg yolks
VEGETABLE OIL

Method

1. Pass the egg whites through a sieve, pressing down with the back of a spoon. Add the corm starch and mix well. Corn starch prevents tearing of the pancake.

2. Heat and grease a small non-stick pan on low heat. Tilt the frying pan slightly and pour the egg white to the higher side of the pan from front to back. Let it run to make the pancake thin.
When the surface is dry, turn over briefly. Remove from the pan and allow to cool.

3. Place the egg yolk and the ½ tsp of water and beat lightly. Now cook as for the egg white.

4. The diamond shape is traditional. Or roll the pastry and cut in strips as preferred.

Golden Pepper Chicken With Onion

(DAK CHIM)

This is a very comforting food, lovely to look at when the depth of its colour and the flavour are intensified by the soy sauce. Use more for brown, less for golden.

Ingredients

SERVES 4

4-5 CHICKEN THIGHS (660g/1.45 lbs)
VEGETABLE OIL
1 medium ONION, peeled,
   cut in half and sliced
2 GARLIC CLOVES, crushed
5 tbsp VINEGAR
1 fresh RED CHILLI, sliced
2 SPRING ONIONS, green part
   only, cut roughly

Marinade:

2 tbsp SOY SAUCE
1 ½ cups WATER
2 tsp grated GINGER
2 tsp SESAME OIL

Method

1. Stir-fry onions with oil in a nonstick pan until translucent. Remove onions from the pan and set aside. Add chicken and later garlic to the pan and cook until golden.

2. Add vinegar and let it sizzle while turning the chicken over a few times until most of the liquid is evaporated.

3. Add the marinade and the onions to the pan and let it simmer with the lid on. Baste frequently while turning the chicken around.

4. Add red chilli and spring onion and cook until the liquid is reduced to a sauce.

If using chopsticks cut the chicken into smaller pieces before serving.

Braised Sea Bass with Chunky Radish

(SENGSON CHIM)

If you like fish but not the fuss, try this dish for which you need to ask your fishmonger to prepare 4 fillets of sea bass. The radish needs to cook longer, but is a wonderful addition to this sea bass treat as well as to mackerel.

Ingredients

SERVES 4

590g/1.3 lbs SEA BASS with skin on
250g RADISH sliced 2 cm/3/4 " thick

SAUCE:

3 ½ cup WATER
5 tbsp SOY SAUCE
1 ¼ tbsp CHILLI FLAKES (coarse

gochugaru)
2 GARLIC CLOVES, crushed
½ thumb size GINGER,
   cut in fine strips
3 SPRING ONIONS, cut roughly
2 tsp SESAME OIL

Method

1. Place the radish in a pot and add the sauce. Bring to the boil in medium high heat. Reduce the heat when it boils vigorously. Let it cook covered until the radish is tender (about 40 minutes).

2. Push the radish to the side and add the fish, skin side up. As it cooks, baste several times. As the water subsides, add the ginger, spring onions and sesame oil. Baste more frequently until the sauce is reduced to half.

Tabletop-grilled Steak & Veg with Tofu

(CHOLPAN GUI)

Very much part of Korean life, this is a fun way to share a sizzling hot meal with friends or the family - and direct from the table. You and your guests all participate in the cooking.

Ingredients

SERVES 4

680g/1 ½ lbs BEEF (ribeye or
   sirloin preferred), cut in 6mm
   /1/4” thick squares

1-2 pack MUSHROOMS
A handful OKRA, blanched
3 slim COURGETTES, slice
   diagonally
1 medium Chinese CABBAGE
   (also known as Napa cabbage).
   Use leafy side, cut 5cm/2”long
4 SPRING ONIONS, cut 5cm/2”long

1 cube (400g/14oz) of medium firm
   TOFU cut in half then in sliced
   1.3 cm/½” thick pieces
½ cup CORN STARCH
VEGETABLE OIL

SAUCE for vegetables:

1/3 cup less salt SOY SAUCE
1/3 cup WATER
1 tbsp SESAME OIL
2 tbsp LEMON JUICE

Method

1. Prepare the vegetables and meat. Cook the rice. While the rice is cooking, coat the tofu pieces with the corn starch and grill lightly in a frying pan. This makes it easier to handle the tofu at the table.

2. Put the vegetables and meat on separate serving plates, drizzling over with a little vegetable oil. Coat the grill with a little oil and place it at the centre of the table. Provide each guest with a plate, chopsticks (or knife and fork), a bowl of rice, sauce for vegetables with small side servings of salt and pepper for dipping the meat.

3. Call your guests with a welcoming glass of wine, allowing about 3 minutes for the grill to heat up. As space becomes available grill further portions, alternating meat and vegetables. Make your guests feel free to help themselves.

Spicy Grilled Pollock
(BUGO GUI)

Lightly browned here and there, this can be either a main dish or side. It's an 'emergency' or easy-to-prepare food *provided* you have a useful collection of Korean basics in your store cupboard! Here I used a hot and sweet marinade and added lemon juice.

Ingredients

SERVES 4

2 whole DRIED POLLOCK (100g/3.5oz), trimmed and cut 5cm/2" long
VEGETABLE OIL

MARINADE:

4 tbsp CHILLI PASTE (*gochujang*)
2 tsp CHILLI FLAKES (*gochugaru*)

1 ½ tbsp SUGAR
1 tbsp GRATED GINGER
1 tbsp LEMON JUICE
4 tsp SOYA SAUCE
2 GARLIC CLOVES, crushed
CHIVES for garnish

Method

1. Prepare the marinade.

2. Soak the dried pollock in water for a few minutes. Hold the pieces in your palms and press out excess water. Spread half of the marinade on both sides using the back of a spoon.

3. Heat a frying pan, drizzle 1-2 spoonfuls of oil and grill the fish until both sides are lightly browned. Drizzle more marinade on top when ready.
Cut chives for garnish.

Serve with rice and non-spicy vegetables.

One-Dish Meals

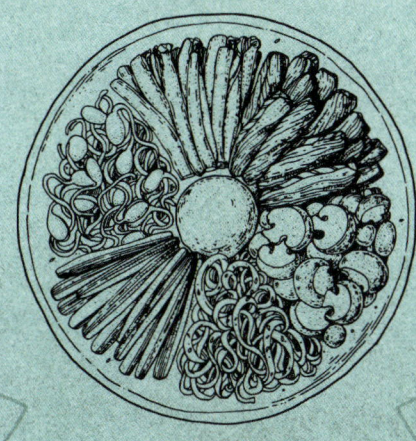

Or vegetarian option
if preferred.

Rub for Flavour
Pork Bibimbap

The most versatile dish in Korean cooking, *'bibim'* comes from the action of the ingredients rubbing with each other when mixed together.

There are endless possibilities for cold or room temperature toppings. For instance you could take out the pork and use any or all of the veg in my book to make vegetarian *'Bibimbap'*.

The beauty of this dish Rub For Flavour is that you can prepare all your veg in advance and serve them at room temperature. Cook the rice in your usual way. But allow it to cool to serve at room temperature (never cold from the fridge).
Pork should be served slightly warm.

Ingredients

SERVES 4

454g/1 lb PORK
3 medium ONIONS, cut in half and sliced
1 pack OYSTER MUSHROOMS,
   tear them
3 medium CARROTS, julienned
1 COURGETTE, cut in strips
VEGETABLE OIL
4 EGGS

MILD SAUCE:

3 tbsp SOY SAUCE
1 tbsp WATER

4 tbsp SESAME OIL
1 tsp toasted SESAME SEEDS

HOT SAUCE:

4 tbsp CHILLI PASTE (*gochujang*)
1 tbsp SESAME OIL
1 tbsp GRATED GINGER
1 tbsp RICE VINEGAR or lemon juice
4 tsp SOY SAUCE
4 tsp SUGAR
2 tsp CHILLI FLAKES (coarse *gochugaru*)
1 GARLIC CLOVE, crushed

▶

Method

1. Heat the frying pan on medium heat. Drizzle a tbsp of oil and stir-fry the onions until slightly brown. Set aside. In the same frying pan, tear the mushrooms and stir-fry keeping the carrots and courgette apart. Courgettes cook very fast. Be careful not to wilt them.

2. Prepare 2 ½ cups rice (see pages 96 & 97). While the rice is cooking, cook the pork in the frying pan. Add salt lightly. Slice the pork thin. Drizzle 2 tsp of the hot sauce and mix well.

Other Suggestions

Mushrooms, carrots,
bean sprouts, acorn jelly,*
spinach, radish salad,
mung bean jelly,*
fried egg

Warm pan grilled fish,
grated carrots, bean
sprouts, egg yolk and
white, cucumber,
avocado, radish sprouts

Serve with a choice of hot and mild sauces

3. Place the rice in individual open bowls and arrange the meat and veg on top. Meat is the only warm ingredient.
Make thin yellow and white pancakes (see *Jidan* page 23) and cut as strips. Or simply fry the eggs and add to each bowl.

4. Leave it to your guests to make their personal choice of hot or mild sauces, or add both.

for Bibimbap

Romaine lettuce, perilla leaves,* cucumber, toasted seaweed,* acorn jelly,* mung bean jelly,*

*Available from many Asian food suppliers (see page 132).

Cool Summer Shrimp Noodles

(BIBIM GUKSU)

This is a wonderful seafood dish set off by the earthy, nutty flavour of buckwheat noodles served cold. As with *Bibimbap* (see page 35), be bold.

Feel free on other occasions to substitute specific meats, fish or vegetables to give an endless variation of tastes.

Ingredients

SERVES 4

340g/12oz BUCKWHEAT NOODLES
1 tbsp SESAME OIL

454 g/1 lb SHRIMPS with
    shells but without the head
1 ½ cups RICE WINE or
    white wine
1 cup WATER
1 pack SHIITAKE mushroom
    or mixed
2 medium COURGETTES,
    cut into strips
3 small CUCUMBERS, cut
    into strips
1 bunch WATER CRESS,
    or chrysanthemum green
4 fried EGGS, or made as

pancakes and sliced

MILD SAUCE:

3 tbsp SOY SAUCE
1 tbsp WATER
3 tbsp SESAME OIL
1 tsp toasted SESAME SEEDS

HOT & SWEET VINAIGRETTE:

3 tbsp CHILLI PASTE (*gochujang*)
1 ½ tbsp RICE VINEGAR or
    lemon juice
1 tbsp SESAME OIL
2 tsp SUGAR
1 GARLIC CLOVE, crushed

Method

1. Rub the crushed garlic around the mild sauce bowl and add the garlic pieces to the hot and sweet vinaigrette. Mix both sauces and set aside.

2. Stir-fry the mushrooms, then the courgette separately. Season lightly with salt and pepper. Prepare the cucumbers and water cress and keep them fresh in the refrigerator.

3. Wash the shrimps with the shells on. Cut the back of the shells with scissors, ▶

then use a knife to cut lightly and remove the vein (dark line). Bring the white wine and water to the boil in a pot and cook the shrimps for 2 minutes until they turn pink. Let cool.

Peel the shells and divide the shrimp in half lengthwise. Set aside.

4. Bring a pot of water to the boil and cook the noodles until tender but still chewy (follow the instruction on the package). Drain the noodles in the sieve and rinse under cold water. Add 1 tbsp sesame oil and mix.

5. Divide the noodles into individual bowls. Arrange all the toppings around it. Prepare the eggs and place on the side. Serve with the sauces.

Leave it to your guests to make their own choice of hot or mild sauce – or add both!

· ·

Another Combination for a Cold Noodle Dish

(BIBIM GUKSU)

Buckwheat noodles, mushrooms,
shrimp, Asian pear, cucumber,
squid, carrots, chrysanthemum greens
or water cress (opposite)', lettuce

Served with hot and mild sauce.

Tofu

AND

More

(BANCHAN – WARM SIDE DISHES)

Usually Korean cooking
is not separated into
starters and mains, but for
convenience I've described
them this way here.
Here are some
warm sides or starters

Ginger & Lemon Crispy Tofu

(DUBU JIJIM)

Another staple of Korean cooking, tofu (we call it dubu) is also packed with protein and was made originally in China around 2,000 years ago. Created by curdling fresh hot soya milk, it's easier to digest than meat sources of protein.

Some regard tofu as having no taste. Plain and unprepared, that may be true… but a delicious flavour is created immediately it takes on spices.

This simple dish is absolutely delicious when the tofu is sizzling hot. Use soft or medium firm tofu; never hard.

Ingredients

SERVES 4

1 cube (400g/14 oz) soft
   or medium firm TOFU
¼ tsp SEA SALT
½ cup CORN STARCH
VEGETABLE OIL

SAUCE:

4 tsp SOY SAUCE
2 tsp SESAME OIL
1/2 tsp GRATED GINGER JUICE
2 tsp LEMON JUICE

Method

1. Cut tofu into half and slice 1.3cm/½" thick. Arrange on a plate. Sprinkle lightly with salt. Leave for 15 minutes.

2. While waiting, prepare the sauce and set aside.

3. Drain liquid from the tofu completely. Coat generously with corn starch on all sides. Don't worry about the lumps: it all becomes crispy.

4. Heat a non stick frying pan, drizzle 2-3 tbsp oil and grill the tofu pieces until crispy. Drizzle the sauce at the bottom of each plate. Place tofu pieces on top. Serve hot. But be careful: grilled tofu can be very hot.

Silken Seasoned Tofu
(YANGNYOM DUBU)

Try this as a first course: it's delicate, yet spicy enough to stimulate the appetite.

You should find silken tofu easy to buy in bigger supermarkets. If not, soft tofu is fine. It may come in different sizes—make a judgement on how much to buy based on the number of eaters—or the appetite of your guests. You can use shop bought chilli flakes.

Ingredients

SERVES 4

2 silken TOFU (300g each)

SAUCE:

1 GARLIC CLOVE, crushed fine
4 tsp SOY SAUCE

4 tsp SESAME OIL
2 tsp toasted SESAME SEEDS,
   crushed with your finger tips
1 tsp CHILLI FLAKES
1 tsp chopped SPRING ONION
   or chives

Method

1. Rub the crushed garlic around the sauce bowl and discard the lumps. Combine the sauce in the same bowl and set aside.

2. Cut the tofu to the chosen portion sizes. Place them in a wide bowl and cover with just boiled hot water for about 3 minutes.

3. Drain the water and place the tofu in separate bowls. Top with the sauce.

Seasoned Tofu with Pollock Roe

(YANGNYOM DUBU) 2

Salted pollock roe is a delicacy in Korea usually eaten with spicy seasonings. Sometimes we add it to savoury steamed egg custard.

Ingredients

SERVES 4

1 ½ silken TOFU (300g each)
  Or 1 cube soft TOFU (400g/14oz)

TOPPING:

6 salted POLLOCK ROE
1 tbsp SESAME OIL

2 tsp toasted SESAME SEEDS
½ tsp CHILLI FLAKES (coarse
  gochugaru)
1 GARLIC CLOVE, crushed fine
1 tsp LEMON JUICE
Cut CHIVES for garnish

Method

1. Squeeze out the pollock roe from the skin into the bowl and sprinkle the seasonings on top. Do not mix too much. Refrigerate to keep cold.

2. When ready to serve, cut the tofu to the chosen portion sizes.

Place them in a wide bowl and cover with just boiled water for 3 minutes.

3. Drain the water and place the tofu on individual bowls. Add a spoonful of topping on each one. The slightly warm tofu and the cold pollock roe are wonderful together. Serve immediately.

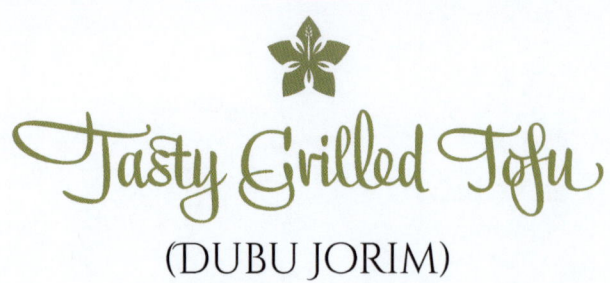

Tasty Grilled Tofu

(DUBU JORIM)

As I say earlier, protein-rich tofu is a big favourite in Korean cooking. It takes on many flavours and is increasingly popular with plant food enthusiasts around the world.

However the bonus is that this recipe makes the tofu, with sesame seeds and chilli, a really easy treat when time is short.

Ingredients

SERVES 4

1 cube (400 g/14 oz) soft or medium firm TOFU, cut in half, then sliced 1.3 cm/ ½"

SAUCE:

4 tsp SOY SAUCE

1 tbsp SESAME OIL

1 ½ tsp toasted SESAME SEEDS, crushed

1 ½ tsp CHILLI FLAKES (coarse *gochugaru*)

2 SPRING ONION, chopped

1 GARLIC CLOVE, crushed fine

Method

1. Prepare the sauce. Heat a large non-stick pan. Drizzle with 1-2 spoonful of oil and sear the tofu pieces until lightly brown on both sides. Then sprinkle the sauce over and let it sizzle until reduced by half.

Serve it warm.

Lemon Grilled Scallops on a Stick

(KWANJA GUI)

Scallops are a highly-prized delicacy here as well as in Korea, and would make a very fine first course. Choose when they're fresh and translucent, not sitting in milky water. The colour changes when cooked. Work with a light touch and don't cook through. Just sizzle briefly on both sides.

Ingredients

SERVES 4

113g/4oz SCALLOPS,
  cut horizontally in half
12 BAMBOO STICKS
VEGETABLE OIL

1/3 LEMON
2 tsp SESAME OIL
COARSE SEA SALT

Method

1. Soak the bamboo sticks in water for 30 minutes. Pierce the scallops with bamboo sticks. Heat a non-stick frying pan, drizzle a little oil and grill until lightly brown on one side (10 seconds).

Turn over and brown again.

2. Arrange on serving plate. Add a dash of lemon juice, sesame oil and a pinch of salt.

Serve immediately.

Skewered Beef with Mushrooms & Carrots

(SANJOK)

Beef and carrots may sound a familiar combination to western ears, but this warming dish has a Korean twist that will appeal to many. Once a meal for special occasions, it can be made easily. So there's no need to wait for that special day.

Try Asian stores for *songii* pine mushrooms (highly prized in Korea), but if not available you can use shiitake or oyster mushrooms. Or even replace the carrots with another vegetable.

Ingredients

SERVES 4

225g/8oz BEEF ribeye or sirloin, cut to finger size
1 large CARROT
3 SPRING ONIONS
5 large SHIITAKE or OYSTER mushrooms (or 2 *songii pine mushrooms*)
6-7 medium length BAMBOO sticks

MARINADE:

4 tbsp SOY SAUCE
1 tbsp WATER
1 GARLIC CLOVE, crushed fine
1 tsp SESAME SEEDS
1 ½ tsp SUGAR
Ground BLACK PEPPER

Method

1. Soak the bamboo sticks in water.
Cut the meat in finger sizes and sprinkle with 1/3 of the marinade.
Cut the vegetables to a similar size as your meat.

2. Steam the carrots until semi-cooked. Blanch the white part of the spring onion and dip in cold water and drain. No need to blanch the green parts.

3. Lightly oil the bamboo sticks and place them through the meat and vegetables. Drizzle a spoonful of oil in a heated non stick frying pan. Grill them lightly brown.

4. Drizzle over half of the marinade while cooking. Let it sizzle until most of the liquid evaporates. Sprinkle more marinade as you serve.

Bean Pancake with Seafood & Bacon

(BINDAETTOK)

This is a very 'homey' and hearty meal with minced pork plus Korea's favourite cabbage side dish *Kimchi*.

A delicate and refined version of this recipe was created by my friend Yuran Lee, a well known Korean artist and food enthusiast. Her simple but inspired idea was to make the pancakes smaller than usual…add seafood and bacon…and chop the ingredients roughly. This enhances the flavour.

We use mung beans which you will find readily available in Asian shops or online.

Ingredients

SERVES 4-5

1 cup skinless MUNG BEANS
  soaked in water 4 hours
4 streaky BACON STRIPS
1 medium ONION, chopped
1/3 cup rough chopped SHRIMPS
½ cup rough chopped SQUID or CLAMS
½ COURGETTE, sliced fine strips
1 GREEN CHILLI (*putgochu*), chopped
2 tsp SALT
1 tsp SUGAR

BLACK PEPPER
VEGETABLE OIL
DILL or other salad green (optional)

SAUCE:

4 tbsp SOY SAUCE
4 tbsp WATER
2 ½ tbsp LEMON JUICE
¼ tsp CHILLI FLAKES (coarse *gochugaru*)

Method

1. First drain the soaked beans. In a blender, lightly grind the beans with 1 ¾ cups water. (Leave a little texture). Transfer to a bowl and set aside.

2. Grill the bacon strips when drained of fat and chopped.

3. Using the bacon pan, save a little fat to cook the the chopped onion.

4. Now add to the mung beans all the prepared ingredients (shrimps plus the squid/clams, bacon, onion, courgette, green chilli, salt and black pepper. Gently mix together. You are now ready to make the pancakes.

5. Heat (medium) a non-stick pan and drizzle 1 ½ spoonfuls oil. Pour out one heaped tbsp of batter per pancake (more if required).

Before the pancakes set, quickly place dill or other attractive greens on top. Turn the pancakes over until also lightly brown. Serve warm.

Beef and Vegetables with Clear Noodles

(JAPCHE)

Thin sliced beef sirloin, and a mix of mushrooms and sweet potato noodles, help to make this a filling meal at any time of the year.

In Korea we especially enjoy it as a treat during the Full Moon Festival (*Chuseok*) celebrating harvest time. The shop-bought noodles are made of a sweet potato starch - good news for many, as they're naturally gluten free. I've used beef in this recipe but make the dish meat-free if preferred.

Always bear in mind that cooked noodles and rice become hard if stored in the refrigerator; so take the chill away in a heated frying pan drizzled over with 2-3 tbsp of water.

Ingredients

SERVES 4

113g/4oz CLEAR NOODLES (*dangmyon*)

SAUCE for the noodles:

2 tbsp SOY SAUCE
2 tbsp WATER
2 tbsp SESAME OIL
1 ½ tbsp SUGAR
BLACK PEPPER

170g/6 oz BEEF SIRLOIN, sliced thin
1 ONION, cut in half and sliced
1 CARROT, cut 4-5cm long and sliced thin
A handful SHIITAKE mushrooms, sliced
½ handful dried BLACK mushrooms
  (optional), soaked in water until soft
1 bunch SPINACH

Method

1. Prepare the meat and vegetables in similar lengths.
2. Season the beef slices with a drop of soy sauce, sesame oil and sesame seeds, and stir-fry lightly. Set aside.
Stir-fry onion slices, mushrooms, carrot slices all separately. Lightly season with sesame oil and salt. Set aside.
3. Wash the spinach gently. Prepare a bowl of ice cold water. Blanch the spinach in boiling water, press down once, immediately remove and immerse it in ice cold water you prepared and drain. Gather it in your palms and squeeze out the excess water. Add a drop of sesame oil and a pinch of salt.
4. Cook the noodles in boiling water until transparent (follow the instruction on the pack). Drain in a sieve, rinse under cold running water and cut the length 2-3 times with scissors.
5. In the same frying pan, drizzle with oil, stir fry noodles with marinade. Mix with beef and vegetables. Serve warm.

Why We Celebrate
Chuseok

(THE FULL MOON HARVEST)

Chuseok means 'autumn evening' and the big day for us is Full Moon Day. It's on the 15th day of the 8th lunar month, usually in September. Older important days follow the lunar calendar such as New Year's Day, Full Moon Day in January (*Daeborum*), the beginning of seasons, *Chuseok*, solstices and so on.

For *Chuseok*, we Koreans take three days off to travel to our home towns and cities for the ceremony of *charae*. Although simplified now, the ceremony was once performed with elaborate displays of food made with the new harvest.

All of this is expressed in movingly-respectful bows to give thanks to our ancestors. After that, the feast is shared with family members. Then we visit the graves of our ancestors. The entire country is bustling.

Beef and vegetables with clear noodles (*Japche* page 58), taro root soup (*Toranguk*) and half moon rice cake steamed with pine needles (*Songpyon*) are the typical foods representing *Chuseok*.

Vegetarian Sides and Kimchi

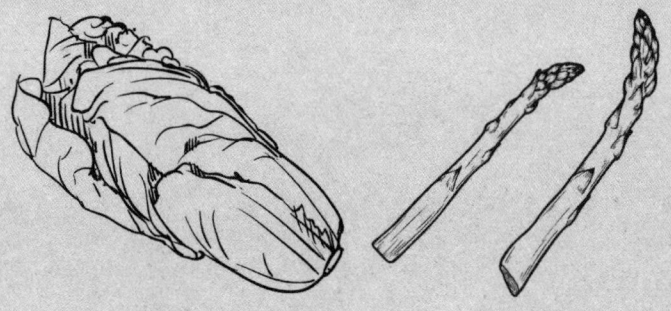

These are small plates, easy to prepare in advance and served cold or at room temperature. Make sufficient to suit your guests. But balance the flavours between hot and mild forcontrast.

*Remember, all vegetables
can be toppings for
Bibimbap (pages 35, 36)*

Steamed Courgette with Seasoned Soy

(HOBAK CHIM)

Koreans usually like vegetables barely cooked - we like to feel the crunch! However tenderness of the courgette is the key to this mildly spiced dish.

Ingredients

SERVES 4

4 small COURGETTE, ends trimmed and cut in half lengthwise

SAUCE:
2 ½ tbsp SOY SAUCE
1 tbsp SESAME OIL

2 tsp toasted SESAME SEEDS
2 tsp CHILLI FLAKES (coarse *gochugaru*)
1 small GARLIC clove, crushed fine
1 tbsp SPRING ONION, chopped

Method

1. Steam the courgette, cut side up until very soft (approximately 7-8 minutes). Young courgettes cook quicker.

2. In the meantime, combine the above ingredients to make the sauce.

3. Transfer the courgettes to a serving plate. Score diagonally a few times, add the sauce on top. Best served warm.

Spicy Asparagus
(ASPARAGUS MUCHIM)

I have chosen asparagus for this recipe instead of *durup*, a spring vegetable. This is due to unavailability outside Korea. The texture and the scent may not be the same, but asparagus or tender stem broccoli is your best alternative. Choose them plump.

Ingredients

SERVES 4

600g/1.3lbs green ASPARAGUS

Seasoned Chilli Paste:

3 tbsp CHILLI PASTE (*gochujang*)
2 tsp CHILLI FLAKES (coarse *gochugaru*)

2 ½ tbsp SESAME OIL
1 tbsp LEMON JUICE
1 tbsp SUGAR
2 tsp toasted SESAME SEEDS
1 small GARLIC CLOVE, crushed fine

Method

1. Season the paste with the ingredients above and set aside.

2. Cut off the rough base of the asparagus. Using a potato peeler, half of the remaining skin should be peeled away from the centre in a downward direction.

3. Steam the asparagus, barely 2 minutes for the plump size. Broccoli may need less time. It should be cooked when checked with a knife, but still firm. Immediately dip briefly into ice cold water and drain. This keeps the bright green colour. Mix with half of the sauce. Drizzle more over the top. Serve cold.

Sweet & Sour Radish Salad

(MUSENGCHE)

Sorry, readers! - make this dish only if you can find Korean or Asian radish, a variety which has a rounder shape and is sweet. It's special and at times even peppery. You should find it translucent and dense without holes.

Cayenne pepper is an acceptable substitute if you do not have chilli powder in hand.

Ingredients

SERVES 4

½ medium size ASIAN RADISH
   (300g/10 ½ oz), sliced and
   cut in fine strips
2 tsp SALT

1 tbsp CHILLI POWDER (*gochugaru*)

1 tbsp RICE VINEGAR or
   white wine vinegar
2 tsp SESAME OIL
2 tsp SUGAR
CHIVES for garnish

Method

1. Sprinkle salt over the cut radish strips and leave for 30 minutes until wilted.

Then hold the strips in your palms and squeeze out the excess water.

Combine with the rest of the spices. Keep in the refrigerator to serve cold. Cut chives for garnish.

Refreshing Seaweed Salad
(MIYOK MUCHIM)

This is a 'sea plant'—seaweed. But *miyok* isn't the seaweed you see on the beach. It's tender and much finer.

There are three varieties we use frequently. *Giim* is a very fine sea plant which is then processed into the shape of a paper-thin sheets. We season with sesame oil and salt, then roast it lightly to wrap the rice. You can find them in Asian shops ready to eat and cut to serving size. So convenient! A larger variety is called *miyok* (or *wakame*). We use this for soup. A thicker variety is kelp (*dashima*), used for flavouring or frying.

In old Korea, sea divers collected *miyok* and *dashima* growing on the rocks in deep seas. These days all are cultivated and dried.

Ingredients

SERVES 4

30g/1oz SEAWEED (*miyok*, also called *wakame*)
VEGETABLE OIL
2 tbsp SESAME OIL

4 tsp SOY SAUCE
1 tsp toasted SESAME SEEDS
1 ½ tbsp LEMON JUICE or VINEGAR
½ LEMON for garnish

Method

1. Soak the *miyok* in lukewarm water for 15 minutes. Let the pieces soften and expand. If long, cut them a few times with scissors. You will have about 3 cups.

2. Heat a frying pan and drizzle a spoonful of oil. Stir-fry the *miyok* in the pan until most of the liquid evaporates (4-5 minutes). Let it cool. Mix with seasonings. Refrigerate for at least 3 hours. Adjust the seasoning and add a dash of fresh lemon juice before serving.

Lemon Spinach with Pepper
(SIGUMCHI NAMUL)

This anytime of the year dish is a tasty and very quick side treat. Spinach has lots of health giving calcium plus, in this recipe, the acidity of a dash of lemon juice. It also gives a touch of refreshing flavour.

Fresh Korean spinach has a naturally sweet flavour but is not generally available here. So the spinach you'll find in the supermarket is a good alternative.

Ingredients

SERVES 4

400g/0.9lb SPINACH
1 GARLIC CLOVE, crushed
4 tsp SESAME OIL
2 tsp SOY SAUCE

2 tsp toasted SESAME SEEDS
A dash of LEMON or lime juice
BLACK PEPPER

Method

1. Wash the spinach gently. Prepare a bowl of ice cold water. Blanch the spinach in boiling water, press down once, remove immediately and immerse it in the ice cold water you prepared. Drain.

2. Gather the spinach in your palms and press out any excess water. Cut the spinach ball in half and keep in the refrigerator until ready to serve.

3. Rub the crushed garlic in the bowl and discard the lumps. In the same bowl, combine the spinach with sesame oil, soy and sesame seeds (crush with your finger tips). Add the dash of lemon or lime juice and black pepper.

Crunchy Bean Sprouts
(SUKJU NAMUL)

This is a delicate, simple and soothing dish. It even looks refined!

Ingredients

SERVES 4

225g/ ½lb BEAN SPROUTS,
   bean skin and tail ends removed
2 tsp SESAME OIL
2 tsp toasted SESAME SEEDS,
   crushed

1 small GARLIC CLOVE,
   crushed fine
SALT and PEPPER
CHIVES for garnish

Method

1. Put the bean sprouts in boiling salted water. Cover the pot for 1-2 minutes. It should be cooked but still crunchy. Spread out on a large plate to cool. When cooled, gather it in your palms and press out the excess water.

2. Refrigerate to serve cold. When you are ready to serve, for extra flavour rub the crushed garlic in a bowl and discard the lumps. Add the bean sprouts to the bowl with seasonings. Add chives for garnish

Nutty Soya Bean Sprouts
(KONG NAMUL)

This dish is full of protein with a nutty taste. It can be time consuming because the tail ends of the bean sprouts need to be removed.

Cayenne pepper is an acceptable substitute if chilli powder isn't to hand.

Ingredients

SERVES 4

225g/½lb SOYA BEAN SPROUTS, bean skins and tail ends removed
2 tsp SESAME OIL

1 GARLIC CLOVE, crushed fine
¼ tsp CHILLI POWDER (*gochugaru*)
SALT & PEPPER
CHIVES for garnish

Method

1. Cook the bean sprouts in boiling salted water for approximately 5 minutes until the yellow heads are cooked. Drain.

2. Spread out on a plate to cool. When cooled, gather in your palms and squeeze out the excess water. Refrigerate to serve cold.

3. When ready to serve, rub the crushed garlic inside the bowl then discard the lumps. Combine the bean sprouts in the same bowl with seasonings.

Add chives for garnish.

Green Chilli Potato Strips

(GAMJA BOKUM)

These look simply elegant on the plate, and spicy green chilli adds a surprise of wonderful flavour to the potato strips. Try this dish as a good addition to *Bibimbap* (page 35). No need to peel if you brush the skin well.

Cutting the potato in finer strips looks attractive on the plate and shortens cooking time.

Ingredients

SERVES 4

2 large POTATOES
VEGETABLE OIL
1-2 GREEN or RED CHILLIS,
 (preferably spicy) sliced

3-4 tbsp WATER
SALT and PEPPER

Method

1. Heat a non-stick pan, drizzle 1-2 tbsp oil and cook the potato strips in a thin layer in the pan. Drizzle 3-4 tbsp water over the potato, add green chilli and cover the pan. You'll hear the sizzle and the steam will help the cooking. *Do not brown.*

2. Gently stir a few more times until cooked tender. Season with salt and pepper. Best when warm but it can also be served at room temperature.

Chrysanthemum Green Salad

(SSUKAT MUCHIM)

You'll love the wonderful scent of this edible vegetable. They can be cooked with seafood or used fresh for salad. Find chrysanthemum greens in Korean, Japanese and Chinese markets. But — *please* — do not confuse them with the chrysanthemums in your garden.

Here I use the marinated chilli paste described in my recipe for Spicy Asparagus.

Ingredients

SERVES 4

2 bunches CHRYSANTHEMUM GREEN

SAUCE:

3 tbsp CHILLI PASTE (*gochujang*)
2 tsp CHILLI FLAKES (coarse *gochugaru*)

2 ½ tbsp SESAME OIL
1 tbsp LEMON JUICE
2 tsp SUGAR
2 tsp toasted SESAME SEEDS
1 small GARLIC CLOVE, crushed fine

Method

1. Remove the stems of the chrysanthemum greens, wash and drain. Refrigerate to serve cold.

2. Combine the sauce with the greens just before eating otherwise it can wilt. When ready, use half of the sauce and mix. Coat the sauce roughly and drizzle more or less depending on your preferred spiciness. Serve cold.

Chilli Cucumber

(OEE NAMUL)

This is a refreshing substitute for Korean's favourite taste experience, *Kimchi* (marinated cabbage). Have it if you would like to try something else when *Kimchi* is not available.

Ingredients

SERVES 4

3 Asian CUCUMBERS, or
  1 regular cucumber.
  Cut in half sliced thin

Sauce:

3 tbsp CHILLI PASTE (*gochujang*)
¾ tbsp CHILLI FLAKES (coarse
  gochugaru)
2 ½ tbsp SESAME OIL

1 tbsp LEMON JUICE
1 tbsp SUGAR
2 tsp toasted SESAME SEEDS
1 small GARLIC CLOVE, crushed fine

Method

1. Mix the sliced cucumber with the sauce just before serving. Be careful: if you mix this too early, salt in the chilli paste will soften the cucumber slices and release the water.

Serve cold.

Chilli Cabbage

(KIMCHI)

There are several vegetables that you can use to form the basis of Korea's big side dish favourite *Kimchi,* but the most popular is cabbage.

A warning: 1) you need about 6 hours to wilt the cabbage with salt; and 2) everything must be prepared about 5 days in advance to ferment and develop a good taste.

Not to worry if you're less patient: quality ready prepared *Kimchi* can be found at most Asian specialty shops or online (see page 132).

Ingredients

SERVES 4 (3-4 SERVINGS)

1 Chinese CABBAGE (1.25 kg/2 ¾ lbs), also known as Napa cabbage
½ cup coarse sea SALT
250g/½lb RADISH, cut fine strips
½ cup CHILLI FLAKES (coarse *gochugaru*)
Thumb size GINGER, grated
3 GARLIC CLOVES, crushed

4 SPRING ONIONS, cut diagonally
2 tbsp small SALTED SHRIMPS, chopped

BINDER for the seasonings:

1 ½ tbsp FLOUR (or sweet rice powder)
1 cup WATER
½ tsp salt

Method

1. Trim the cabbage and wash the outer leaves. Slice the base into 4 equal parts to a depth of about 10 cm. Then pull apart.

2. From your ½ cup of coarse salt (or kosher salt), add 3 tbsp with 3 cups of water in a suitable bowl. ▶

Now, one at a time, place the cut pieces of cabbage in the bowl and soak them individually in the salt water. Using the rest of the salt, sprinkle between each stem but less on the leaves. Repeat for all pieces.

Some of the cabbage will be sitting in the salt water. Be sure to rotate at least once during the 6 hours of wilting.

3. The white of the leaves is now softer. Wash thoroughly twice. Put down the cut side and drain.

4. Make the binder in a small saucepan combining the flour (or sweet rice powder) and the water. Cook over medium heat stirring constantly to avoid lumps. When thickened, remove from the hob and let cool.

5. Combine the cut radish, chilli flakes, ginger, garlic, spring onion, salted shrimps and cooled binder.

6. Place the mixture between the cabbage leaves. Cut the 2 larger outer leaves and set aside. Put the prepared marinated cabbage in a large jar. Press down any air pockets between each piece. Use the 2 leaves to cover the contents before closing the jar.

7. Keep your *Kimchi* for two days at room temperature to commence fermenting. It takes less time in a hot climate, more when cold.

Note that as the mixture ferments the juice will begins to rise to the top of the *Kimchi*.

At this point, refrigerate where it will ferment further and develop its taste in about 3 days.

After this time remove the top cover. Take out a portion and cut it in bite sizes.

Always replace the cover to protect the taste.

Apart from p. 85's chilli cabbage recipe (pictured left), this popular Korean side dish can be made with such alternatives as radish (below), cucumber and others.

White Kimchi

(BAEK KIMCHI)

Here is a simple White Kimchi recipe without using chilli flakes, so it's not spicy. Just fresh red chilli is added for a kick.

Make it about 5 days before you want to eat. This is just a guide.

Ingredients

SERVES 4

1 Chinese CABBAGE (1.25 kg / 2 ¾ lbs)	1 thumb size GINGER, cut in fine strips
½ cup coarse SEA SALT	4 SPRING ONIONS, cut diagonally
250g / ½lb RADISH, cut fine strips	2 fresh red CHILLIS, sliced thin diagonally
3 GARLIC CLOVES: crushed fine	A handful PINE NUTS

Method

1. Follow the steps 1, 2 and 3 of the *Chilli Cabbage Kimchi* (page 85). Instead of 6 hours of wilting with salt, it will take 4-5 hours but the cut pieces will be fresher. Now wash thoroughly twice and drain.

2. Combine the radish, garlic, ginger, spring onion, fresh red chillis and pine nuts. Season with a pinch or two of salt.

3. Place the mixture in between the cabbage stems and leaves. Cut 2 outer leaves and set aside. Put the marinated cabbage in a large jar. Lightly press them down any air pockets between each piece. Use the 2 leaves to cover the contents. Add ½ cup of water to the bowl in which you mixed the garlic, season with 1 ½ tsp coarse salt and dissolve. Pour the liquid over the *Kimchi*, which should be salty when you taste it.

4. Close the lid and leave at room temperature for 2 days to commence fermenting. Once the liquid rises to the top of the *Kimchi*, refrigerate for it to ferment further and develop its taste in about 3 days. When serving, set aside the two covering leaves, take out a portion and cut it to bite sizes. *Always replace the cover to protect the taste.*

The Kimchi Story

You'll find many references to '*Kimchi*' when you explore the wonderful world of Korean cooking. Mostly made using cabbage, it is just a side dish so there are alternatives if it is not to your taste. However we regard the importance of *Kimchi* as being able to make or break the meal!

We Koreans may smile when we say we can't survive without *Kimchi*. But many of us still mean it …

Essentially, in *Kimchi*, the cabbage is marinated with chilli flakes (coarse *gochugaru*), plus garlic, ginger, spring onion, salted little shrimps and salted anchovies. It is then fermented. At times, a few small pieces of fish or oysters add an even deeper flavour. There are many different seasonal varieties and each region has its own specialties.

Kimchi needs to be made at least five days before you will want to eat it and I like it best when it turns slightly sour.

I remember vividly winter days tasting my grandmother's home made wrapped *Kimchi (Bossam)*. I could hold it in the open palm of my hand wrapped in 2-3 leaves of crunchy cabbage. Thumb sized fish chunks, thin sliced chestnuts, pear slices and pine nuts were the highlights. Elegant and refined, my grandmother's food was prepared with attention and style even with the simplest ingredients from her well stocked kitchen. An absolute treat. I loved it.

When *Kimchi* is overripe (very sour) we even make it as a stew with tofu or pork meat. Or add to dumplings or enjoyable savoury pancakes. The possibilities are endless!

In times gone by it was even the done thing to keep big ceramic pots underground to store the *Kimchi* during the cold of a whole winter. These days the traditional ritual is not necessary. If in a hurry, commercial varieties are widely available in Asian stores or online (see page 132).

My Grandmother, My Inspiration

During the worst days of the Korean War my family fled Seoul and travelled to the quiet safety of my grandpa's village. There, as a little girl, I walked past rice paddies on the long journey to school.

My grandma was an amazing cook who created delicious meals with simple ingredients. I admired her very much and once asked her the secret of her cooking. 'Good seasoning!', she said. Of course! Good seasoning lifts good food. Creating and re-creating my own would become a lifetime pleasure.

Growing up, learning different recipes, I often think of my grandma's style and simplicity for inspiration.

Life moved on from those simple childhood days. After university in Seoul I followed my artistic ambition by training at a New York fashion school, then as a career woman heading production for a French fashion company in Hong Kong.

Ultimately I decided to return to New York to raise my young daughter Tai when — *suddenly!* — it happened.

Desperate to improve my domestic cooking skills, and bored by my limited repertoire, I studied at a New York restaurant school. After school I worked long but happy hours helping prepare food for rich and famous clients of the prestigious events company Glorious Food.

It was a moment of awakening. *Food would be my fulfilment, too*. Why hadn't I learned more from grandma?!!

I went on to take short courses at famous cooking schools in France and Italy, and in Korea where my family took care of Tai.

Be inspired: I was nearly 40 when my interest in food renewed not only my life, but a returned passion for the cooking of my native Korea. I had become a featured columnist for the New York edition of the *Korea Times*. And I poured my heart into the writing of earlier books.

All over the world there are so many of us who aspire to the art of appetising food preparation even in the simplest of our dishes. It may be the shortest of arts, gone within minutes. But eaten alone, or shared, the love of preparing good food well can be one of the greatest joys in life.

Preparing Rice

FAST AND SLOW

Do you use rice regularly in your cooking? Sadly it's often unappreciated in many food styles in the West, although there are obvious exceptions.

The wonderfully filling *paellas* of Spain, for instance. Or the Italian favourite *risotto*. Or that childhood favourite rice pudding.

Fast Rice

Ingredients

SERVES 2

1 cup RICE
1 ½ cups WATER

Method

1. Wash the rice in a swirling motion, changing the water several times until clear. Use a sieve to drain the water then transfer it to a medium size pot. Add 1 ½ cups of fresh water, cover and bring to the boil with a medium high heat.

2. Be careful not to let the pot boil over: raising the lid slightly allows the water to settle and be further absorbed by the rice. While the bubbles are subsiding, cover the pot and reduce the heat to low for 5-6 minutes. Turn off and leave for another 10 minutes. It steams inside to complete the cooking.

3. Wet a wooden spoon and fluff to serve.

Fast and Slow

You can have fun using rice in Korean dishes and in Korea we choose short grain which isn't fussy to prepare.

Here are my methods for short grain rice in a hurry, or the slower version (because of the soaking). You may feel this is tastier. It's easier with a glass cover to see what's happening.

Slower But Tastier

Ingredients

SERVES 2

1 cup RICE, soaked in water for 30 minutes
1 cup 2 tbsp WATER

Method

1. Wash the rice in a swirling motion. Change the water several times until clear. Then soak for 30 minutes.

2. Use a sieve to drain the rice then transfer it to a medium size pot. Add 1 fresh cup 2 tbsp of water, cover and bring to the boil with medium high heat. *Do not open the lid during the cooking time.*

3. About 7-8 minutes later, as the bubbles subside, turn the heat to medium. Turn off after 5 minutes. Do not move the pot but allow it to settle for another 10 minutes.

4. Wet a wooden spoon and fluff to serve.

Soups
AND
Porridge

Soups are served
together with rice,
never as a first course

Birthday Soup

(MIYOK GUK)

There's a nutritious Korean cooking seaweed soup, *Miyok Guk*, which is part of our tradition of caring for new mothers in the first few weeks. We believe this soup cleanses the blood and — with health giving calcium and iodine — helps the flow of milk for new born babies.

So revered is *Miyok Guk*, we now continue the tradition by enjoying it on our birthdays and other occasions.

The 'vegetable' in question is a form of seaweed. If that deters you remember that seaweed bread (lava bread) has long been an historic favourite in Wales and many other countries.

Try it at any time! You'll may be pleasantly surprised.

Ingredients

SERVES 4

15g/½ oz SEAWEED (*Miyok also called Wakame*)

100g/3½ oz RIB EYE or beef brisket, sliced thin

1 GARLIC CLOVE, crushed fine

1 tbsp SESAME OIL

5 cups BEEF BONE BROTH (page 104) or kelp broth (page 107)

2 SPRING ONIONS, chopped

SOY SAUCE, salt to adjust seasoning

Ground BLACK PEPPER

Method

1. Take a handful of *miyok*, soak in lukewarm water until tender (15 minutes). Then drain. If long, cut it several times lengthwise.

2. Combine the *miyok* with beef, garlic, sesame oil in a pot. Stir-fry for about 1 minute.

3. Add beef bone broth (page 104) or kelp broth (page 107) and boil gently for about 15-20 minutes until the sliced meat and the *miyok* are tender. Add the spring onions. Adjust seasoning with soy sauce and salt but be careful not to make it too dark.

New Year's Day Beef Soup

(TTOKGUK)

This lovely and filling hot soup is a big favourite in Korea for our lunar New Year's Day in late January or early February. Beef bone broth, rice cake and spring onions give a great kick to the flavour.

Make sure to bring the egg to room temperature before beating it and adding to the soup. A warning though: cold egg will make the broth murky rather than in smooth attractive thin ribbons. The all-rice cake described is available frozen from most Asian stores.

Ingredients

SERVES 4

6 cups BEEF BONE BROTH (page 104)
500g/1 lb sliced RICE CAKE
1 GARLIC CLOVE, crushed
2-3 SPRING ONIONS, cut diagonally

SOY SAUCE, SALT to adjust seasoning
1 EGG, beaten
2 pack toasted thin SEAWEED (*giim*)
BLACK PEPPER

Method

1. Prepare the beef bone broth in advance. Make sure the egg is at room temperature. Prepare the rice cake. If purchased frozen, soak the slices in water for 10 minutes and drain.

2. Bring the broth to the boil, add garlic and rice cake slices. Gently simmer until tender. Adjust the seasoning with salt and just a small amount of soya sauce. This gives flavour without making it too dark.

3. Cut the seaweed in thin strips and set aside.

4. Add the spring onions, cook for 2 minutes. Reduce the heat, swirling with chopsticks or a spoon while slowly adding the beaten egg. Immediately turn off the heat.

Pour the soup in individual bowls and top with the sliced *giim* (seaweed).

Beef Bone Broth

(GOMGUK)

If you can spare the time be prepared for several hours of dedication to this wonderful winter warmer. It's well worth it. In a hurry? Boil once!

Ingredients

TO MAKE ABOUT 11-12 CUPS

1.7kg/3¾lbs BEEF SOUP BONES
1 large ONION, quartered
2 GARLIC CLOVES

1 large LEEK
1 CELERY STALK

Method

1. Cover the bones with water in a pot for 30-40 minutes. Bring to the boil. The top is covered with a brownish foam, so turn off the heat immediately and throw away the water. Wash the bones under cold running water and clean the pot.

2. Cover the bones with fresh water to reach about 2½ cm /1") above and bring to a boil again. Now reduce the temperature, cover and simmer for about 5½ - 6 hours. Remember to add more water to cover the bones to the original level. Eventually the broth will become milky

3. Between 4-4½ hours later, lightly brown the onion in a pan with a spoonful oil and add to the pot with garlic, leek and the celery. Simmer the broth for a further 60 minutes.

4. Squeeze out the garlic, onion, leek, celery stalk and discard. Transfer the broth to a bowl.

5. Re-boil the bones with trimmings. Simmer for 5 hours. Now add the broth to provide a wonderful hearty soup base, freezing part of the base for later use if you wish. The marrowbone is delicious and nutritious. But don't serve marrow directly to guests; they may think it's fat!

Our Festive Dish for a Special Occasion

The delicious and soothing rice cake soup, *Ttokguk* (page 102), is one of the many family feasts we prepare for special moments. The biggest of these is our own New Year's Day which we celebrate according to the Lunar Calendar.

Dressed in traditional costume we give *Sebae* (meaning to bow ceremonially) to our parents and grandparents. We wish them a Happy New Year, and in return they lovingly present the small children of the family with good luck pouches with money inside.

This young family celebrates a traditional festive family occasion.

Ancient legend describes how Buddha designated each year to the 12 animals which came to his birthday feast. As his gift to them, he decided that each one should be honoured for all time in a continuing cycle of 12 years.

For this reason the children born in that year of the cycle are said to have the characteristics of that animal.

Even to this day we have the Year of the Horse, the lamb, monkey, rooster, dog, pig, rat; and the cow, tiger, rabbit, dragon and snake.

Who knows?! You maybe a monkey, a tiger or a rabbit. Or even a rat! To find out, look for your particular year online.

Tofu Stew With Beef Bone Broth

(DUBU CHIGAE)

For the hearty essence of this flavoursome stew I use Beef Bone Broth (page 104). You'll also find that the rich in-depth flavour of this meal is at its best when it's a little on the salty side.

Tofu and green chilli are 'must' ingredients. If you use silken tofu, spoon in big chunks for a look that's far more appetising.

Ingredients

SERVES 4

4 tbsp SOY BEAN PASTE (*denjang*)
2 cups BEEF BONE BROTH (page 104)
1 small ONION, cut roughly
2 GARLIC CLOVES, crushed
4 SHIITAKE mushrooms, cut roughly
1 medium POTATO, cut cubes

½ medium COURGETTE, cut cubes
1 GREEN CHILLI, sliced
¼ tsp CHILLI FLAKES (coarse *gochugaru*)
½ cube SOFT TOFU (200g) or
   1 silken tofu (300g/10.5oz)
1 SPRING ONION, chopped

Method

1. Prepare 2 cups beef bone broth in a bowl. Put the soy bean paste in a sieve and immerse it in the liquid. Press down with the back of a spoon until dissolve. Set aside.

2. Heat a medium pot, add a spoonful of oil and stir fry the onions until lightly browned here and there. Add garlic and stir a few more times.

3. Add the bean paste water and potato cubes and mushrooms followed by courgette cubes. Cook until the potatoes are soft.

4. Add tofu, green chilli, a dash of chilli flakes and cook until boiling. Gently boil for 5 minutes. Mix with spring onion and serve hot.

Spinach Clam Soup
(JOGAE SIGUMCHI GUK)

Traditionally this warming soup uses Korean spinach which is short and has a sweet flavour. However the fresh spinach leaves found in most local food shops make a good alternative.

This calcium rich vegetable goes very well with the taste of soybean paste (*denjang*). Fresh clams from a good fishmonger add a great flavour of the sea. You'll also need to make up the kelp broth described on page 109.

Ingredients

SERVES 4

3 dozen small CLAMS

5 cups KELP BROTH (page 107)

2 bunches SPINACH (300g)

3 tbsp SOY BEAN PASTE (*denjang*)*

1 GARLIC CLOVE, crushed

2 GREEN CHILLIES (*putgochu*), sliced

A dash of CHILLI FLAKES (coarse *gochugaru*)

Method

1. Rinse the clams under the tap then soak in lightly salted water for 40-50 minutes. Cut off the end of the spinach base and wash.

2. Put 5 cups of my kelp broth (below) in a pot. In a sieve, combine soybean paste (*denjang*) then immerse in the kelp broth. Press down the paste with the back of a spoon until it dissolves.

3. Bring the soya bean paste broth to the boil. Add garlic and green chilli.

4. Add the spinach and clams. Remove from the heat as soon as they open. Add a dash of chilli flakes before you serve.

. . . .

Kelp Broth

(DASHIMA KUKMUL - SOUP BASE)

Ingredients

SERVES 4

2 palm size KELP (thick seaweed)

4 dried SHIITAKE MUSHROOMS

6 dried ANCHOVIES, gutted

Method

1. Do not wash the kelp - leave the natural white coating as is. In a pot, soak the pieces together with dried anchovies and dried shiitake mushrooms in lukewarm water for 1 hour.

2. After soaking, bring the broth to boiling point. Continue at boiling point for 10 minutes. Turn off. Remove any foam from the top. Remove the kelp and mushrooms both of which can be sliced thin and used later for flavouring. The anchovies have given sufficient flavour and are no longer required. Now your soup base is ready.

Cold Seaweed Soup with Cucumber
(MIYOK NENGGUK)

Many Asian stores stock *Daesang brand miyok* seaweed (also know as *wakame*) which I use to make this, one of my favourite soups in hot weather.

Served cold, it's so refreshing and appetising when combined with cucumber and just a touch of vinegar. Kelp broth (see page 107) can also add good flavour.

Ingredients

SERVES 4

A handful (29g/1oz) DRIED
   SEAWEED (*miyok - wakame*)
   soaked in water 15 minutes
1 small CUCUMBER, cut
   diagonally in fine strips
3 cups cold KELP BROTH (page 107)
3 tbsp RICE VINEGAR or
   white wine vinegar
1 tbsp SOY SAUCE

1 chopped SPRING ONION
1 GARLIC CLOVE, crushed fine
½ tsp toasted SESAME SEEDS,
   crushed

Method

1. After soaking the seaweed cut approximately 5cm/2" long with scissors. Blanch in boiling water. Immediately dip in cold water and drain.

2. Rub the crushed garlic clove in a bowl and discard the lumps. Combine all the ingredients in the same bowl. Keep in the refrigerator to serve cold. Add sesame seeds before serving.

Porridge with Pine Nuts

(JAATJUK)

This delicate, refined dish is often given to patients in Korea to aid their quick recovery. The pine nuts create a nutritious delicious flavour which really is like butter melting in the mouth. For a smooth consistency, continue to stir while cooking.

Ingredients

SERVES 2

½ cup short grain RICE, washed, soaked in water for 30 minutes, drained
¼ cup PINE NUTS, brown caps removed

¼ tsp SALT
A few PINE NUTS for garnish
HONEY to taste

Method

1. Place the soaked rice and pine nuts in a mixer with 3 cups of water and process until smooth (2 minutes).

2. Put the rice liquid in a pot and bring to the boil. Stir constantly. Reduce the heat to medium high while it thickens, and cook for 5-6 minutes more while stirring. Add salt and garnish with pine nuts. Serve warm.

Add honey to taste.

*Another easy suggestion to add to this true Korean experience: use shop bought seasoned toasted seaweed (*Giim*), slice thin and sprinkle on top.

Fresh Fruit Desserts

TO CLEANSE THE PALATE

For a truly Korean experience I suggest you give your guests just fresh fruit after the meal. The spiciness of our food on your palate is refreshed by the taste of honey and lime, water melon, oranges and the like. Traditional sweet desserts are sometimes served, but only for extra-special occasions. Here I suggest some with my own personal twist.

Honey Persimmon and Lime

(DAN GAAM)

Persimmon fruit is not only a symbol of autumn in Korea, it's a colourful and amazing source of vitamins A, C, B plus essential minerals. Fat free, delicious, and packed with fibre - I absolutely love it. There are two kinds. One is round, pointed and soft inside; the other, (which I prefer) is flat on top and medium firm.

If the fruit is hard, be patient and let it ripen at room temperature for 2-3 days. This recipe is simplicity itself. My personal extra is to add a dressing of honey with lime to give sweetness and citrus. Delicious!

Ingredients

SERVES 4

5 PERSIMMONS flat shape   ½ LIME
2 tbsp HONEY

Method

1. Peel the skin and remove the base of each fruit. Divide into 4.

2. Drizzle over the honey and the lime juice.

Summer Watermelon Smoothie
(WHACHE)

This zingy thirst quencher is the cool drink of choice during Korea's hot summers. Usually just sugar is added, but here I have made a little twist with lime juice. It adds an excitingly refreshing touch. Lemon is acceptable but given the choice, lime is my own favourite.

Ingredients

SERVES 4

½ WATERMELON de-seeded
¾ cup LIME JUICE (6 limes)
¼ APPLE, cored sliced thin

¾ cup SUGAR
Dash of RUM (optional)

Method

1. Scoop out the watermelon. Discard the seeds and purée the pulp in a blender (6 cups purée). *Do not* add water. Refrigerate for 2-3 hours until very cold.

2. Add the lime juice and sugar.

A nice touch might be to use a cookie cutter for the apple slices to make any shape you want. If not, it still tastes as good! Place the pieces on top of the purée. Throw in a dash of rum (or not) as preferred.

Baked Sweet Sweet Potato

(GOON GOGUMA)

As said previously, sweet desserts don't usually figure highly on Korean menus. Apples, peaches or other fruit help to clean the palate.

However you may like this combination of the fibre of sweet potatoes, dark brown sugar and melting butter.

Ingredients

SERVES 4

4 medium SWEET POTATOES   2 tbsp DARK BROWN SUGAR
2 tbsp BUTTER

Method

1. Heat the oven to 190°C/375°F. Wash the sweet potatoes, line up on a tray and bake for about 45-50 minutes or until soft.

2. Tear open the skin on one side of each sweet potato and fluff the flesh with a fork.

3. Add a knob of butter on each and sprinkle dark brown sugar. Serve hot.

Tangy Orange with Fruit Preserve

(YUJACHONG ORANGE)

Jeju Island is situated on the south west tip of the Korean Peninsula and is famous for its super healthy women divers. These amazing women can stay in the water for many hours, diving for up to three minutes at a time to gather delicious but hard to find shellfish.

However just as famous on the island is *Yujachong**, a delicate tea sweetener made from a wonderfully scented local citrus fruit called Yuja.

Yujachong was my inspiration to add 5 or 6 peeled, separated whole oranges and a refreshing garnish of mint. It's delicious as a treat with any meal or as a wake-up spread for breakfast rolls or toast.

Ingredients

SERVES 4

5-6 ORANGES
½ cup *YUJACHONG*

MINT for garnish

Method

1. Peel the oranges and cut out the segments. Refrigerate 2-3 hours until very cold. Divide into serving bowls and spread over 1 round tbsp. *Yujachong* according to taste.

*To buy *Yujachong* your best bet is from larger Korean or ethnic food stores or on Amazon. Choose a brand with more of the chunky *Yuja* pieces. It may be listed as 'Honey Citron Tea'.

Chestnuts with Dates and Sweet Rice

(YAKSIK)

A common belief in Korea is that honey and dates have the power to soothe and heal the body. Since they are used in this dessert to sweeten the rice, we call it 'medicinal food' which is the literal translation of the word *Yaksik*. In this case I've made it more delectable as a dessert by increasing the quantity of chestnut and dates. Rice is added as a binding agent. It is essential to use a nonstick sauce pan or pot.

Ingredients

SERVES 4

180g/0.4 lb ready cooked and peeled CHESTNUTS

4 Medjool DATES, seeded and quartered (or 12 dried red dates, soaked in water for 30 minutes)

2 heaped tbsp PINE NUTS, brown caps removed

1 tbsp dark brown SUGAR

½ tsp CINNAMON

1 round tbsp HONEY

½ cup short grain SWEET RICE

¾ cup WATER

Method

1. Wash the rice in a swirling motion until the water is clear. Add the water and wait 30 minutes while preparing other ingredients. Put all the dry ingredients together and set aside.

2. Cook the rice on a medium high heat. When it boils vigorously, lower the heat to medium and add cinnamon and honey with all the dry ingredients. Sprinkle 1 tbsp water over them and cover. Turn off the heat 5 minutes later and let it sit for 10 minutes to finish cooking.

3. Grease a wooden spoon and mix together while still warm. The mixture is ready to to be pressed in any shape you choose. Oil the inside of a small cup with sesame oil, fill it with the *Yaksik*, gently press then remove by turning the cup upside down. Serve at room temperature.

Red Bean Purée with Sweet Rice Balls

(PATJUK)

In Korea this dish is served at the time of the winter Solstice, which has the shortest day and the longest night. Traditionally we consider this the start of preparation for the New Year. *Patjuk* - the red bean porridge - was served to prevent bad luck.

Of course most people no longer think of certain foods as preventing bad luck. But in a country with 5,000 years of history, it's a tradition close to our hearts.

I have varied my recipe for this dessert slightly from the traditional to make it sweeter and tastier.

Ingredients

SERVES 4

1 cup RED BEANS, soaked
  over night in water
2/3 cup SUGAR
A pinch of SALT

½ cup SWEET RICE POWDER
  (*Asian stores*)
4-5 tbsp WARM WATER

Method

1. Cook the soaked beans in a pot/pan with 3 cups of water until the beans are very soft. The liquid should cover the beans during the entire cooking process (approximately 1 hour) adding more water if necessary. While still warm, add sugar and a pinch of salt and use a hand blender to purée the beans until smooth.

2. Put the sweet rice powder in a round bowl, add 4-5 tbsp warm water and mix together using a fork. Form this into small balls the size of your finger tips circling them in your palms.

3. Cook the rice balls in boiling salt water for approximately 6-7 minutes. Their volume increases while cooking. Warm up the bean purée and add the rice balls. Serve warm or at room temperature.

How It All Began

For a better understanding of Korean food it's interesting to know that in ancient times, there were three distinctive ways of cooking. Each related to social status.

The dishes of the King and his royal court were *opulent* and *elaborate*. Commoners, on the other hand, had *simple ingredients* from the crops they produced. Eventually the food of the royals became our biggest influence for special occasions and traditional feast days.

However in general the bold and hearty food flavours of the people have come to predominate in Korean daily life and our ever-popular street food.

Buddhist temple cuisine is another distinctive style which still survives as a big influence in Korean cooking. It connects back to the *Seon* form of Buddhism which reached Korea in the year 372 from the Qin Dynasty of China.

A wholesome religion, the ultimate goal of Buddhism is to reach a heavenly state of mind by self discipline. It was a philosophy which blended well with the nature worship of Shamanism at that time.

Buddha himself did not forbid the eating of meat. However *Seon* Buddhism discouraged the killing of animals for eating purposes and so vegetarian food was prepared for the altar.

One way or another, these delicious food style spread across Korea using vegetables, herbs and other plants from the mountains, plus potatoes. These had been introduced from China in the 1800's and of course, originally South America via England's Sir Walter Raleigh.

Pine nuts were added to a non-spicy version of our traditional favourite, *Kimchi*, and pine needles to *Songpyun* (a rice cake with sweet filling) for aroma.

Ssam (fresh lettuce or steamed courgette leaves wraps) and the frying of kelp (thick sea plant) also originated from temple cuisine. Teas were brewed with edible flowers or roasted grains such as barley, brown rice and corn.

Without any doubt, all have made a lasting influences on Korean food today.

Your Must-Have

Get off to a good start with your interest in Korean cooking by investing in all or some of the ingredients I describe in these pages. Most Asian stores will stock them, or you can also find them online. A useful list for many suppliers of these Korean ingredients can be found on page 132.

SEASONINGS

SOY SAUCE: This is a fermented sauce of soya beans and salt. Use a reduced salt version if preferred. For coeliacs, buy gluten free Tamari sauce.

SEA SALT: My own preference, and a natural source of minerals.

SESAME OIL: A ready made nutty, very aromatic oil squeezed when the seeds were roasted.

SESAME SEEDS: Must be roasted for flavour. Dry roast ½ cup of seeds in a pan over medium heat. Stir slowly at

Korean Store Cupboard

the beginning. As the colour changes, stir constantly until lightly golden. Remove from the heat but continue to stir a minute more because the pan is still hot. Store when cooled. *Break with your finger tips as you season*.

CHILLI or RED PEPPER PASTE: (*gochujang*): Fermented spicy paste of chilly powder, sticky (sweet) rice, soybeans, malt (*yeotgirum*) and salt.

CHILLI FLAKES or COARSE RED PEPPER POWDER (*gochugaru*): Dried and pulverised flakes which give pungent flavour to the dish. If you have a choice, buy the spiciest version.

RICE VINEGAR: Or use white wine vinegar.

GARLIC: Once peeled it can be kept in a jar. But not chopped garlic – it develops a bitter taste.

SPRING ONION: Don't cut off the roots. They last longer if retained.

GINGER: Choose smaller pieces at the grocery shop as they will be younger and tender. When you want to peel, use a teaspoon to scrape the skin. Especially good for pork and fish. Best added near the end of cooking.

This is an abbreviated list but note that many cities have Asian (Chinese, Japanese, Thai) markets with Korean or other suitable products. Many maybe available online.

LONDON

DURI MART

• 10 Station Parade, Uxbridge Rd. Ealing Common, London W5 3LD
Tel: 020 8752 1766

OSEYO

has several stores around central London.

• Soho: 73 – 75 Charing Cross Rd, West End, London WC2H 0NE
Tel: 020 3973 9701

• Waterloo: 158 Waterloo Rd, Bishops, London SE1 8SB
Tel: 020 3417 2690

• Camden: 158 Camden High St., Camden Town, London NW1 0NE
Tel: 020 3105 4857

• 115 Tottenham Court Rd, Bloomsbury, London W1T 5AH
Tel: 020 7388 0160

• Angel: 15 Liverpool Rd, London N1 0RW
Tel: 020 7278 4291

SEOUL PLAZA

• 52 Tottenham Court Rd., Bloomsbury, London W1T 2EH
Tel: 020 7580 4189

• 17 Golders Green Rd., Golders Green, London NW11 8DY
Tel: 020 8209 3739

HMART

• Unit 1, Leigh Close, New Malden, KT3 3NW
Tel: 020 3274 2020
Online shopping, *hmart.co.uk*

KOREA FOOD

• Wyvern Industrial Estate, 4 Unit 5, Beverly Way, New Malden KT3 4PH
Tel: 020 8949 2238
Online shopping, *koreafoods.co.uk*

SEOUL PLAZA

• 126 Malden Rd, New Malden KT3 6DD
Tel: 020 8942 9552

• 36 High St, New Malden KT3 4HE
Tel: 020 8949 4329

ABERDEEN

• Matthews Foods
136-138 Causewayend,
Aberdeen AB25 3TN
Tel: 0122 463 6060

BIRMINGHAM

• Seoul Plaza
536 Bristol Rd,
Birmingham B29 6BD
Tel: 0121 472 2331

BOURNEMOUTH

• Seoul Plaza
6 Cardigan Rd,
Bournemouth BH9 1BJ
Tel: 0120 252 7177

BELFAST

• Asia Supermarket
40 Ormeau Embankment,
Belfast BT6 8LU
Tel: 028 9032 6396

Buy A-Z

BRISTOL

- Dano Mart (Korean)
214 Cheltenham Rd,
St. Andrews,
Bristol BS6 5QU
Tel: 011 7924 6564

- Oriental Market (Korean)
13 Gloucester Rd., Bishopston,
Bristol BS7 8AA
Tel: 011 7942 5002

CAMBRIDGE

- Seoul Plaza
91-93 Mill Rd,
Cambridge CB1 2AW
Tel: 012 2330 3610

CANTERBURY

- Starry Mart
2 Broad Oak House,
Canterbury CT2 7SN
Tel: 012 2776 8804

CARDIFF

- Cardiff Korean & Japanese Food
116 Woodville Rd,
Cardiff CF24 4EE
Tel: 029 2022 3225

COLCHESTER

- Starry Mart
143 Callum Dr, Colchester,
CO2 8FN
Tel: 012 0686 5438
Online shopping, *starrymart.co.uk*

COVENTRY

- Seoul Plaza
Unit 13-14,
Cannon Park shopping center,
Coventry CV4 7EH
Tel: 024 7669 3862

EDINBURGH

- Hua Xing
48-50 Ratcliffe Terrace, Edinburgh
EH9 1ST
Tel: 0131 662 9892

- Matthew's Foods
36 Ingrid Green Rd, Edinburgh
EH14 2ER
Tel: 0131 443 8686

- Superior Oriental
84-86 S Clerk St, Newington,
Edinburgh EH8 9PT
Tel: 0131 667 6667

GLASGOW

- See Woo
29 Saracen St, Glasgow G22 5HT
Tel: 0116 270 1599

LEICESTER

- L-Mart Korea
192 Welford Rd, Leicester LE2 6BD
Tel: 0845 078 8818

LIVERPOOL

- Chung Wah Supermarket
Hardy St, Liverpool L1 5JN
Tel: 0151 707 8488

MANCHESTER

- Oseyo
8 Oxford Rd, Manchester M1 5QA
Tel: 0161 237 3988

OXFORD

- Seoul Plaza
59-63 Cowley Rd, Cowley,
Oxford OX4 1HR
Tel: 018 6524 8191

SWANSEA

- Oriental Express Asian Food Store
89 Brynymor Rd, Swansea SA1 4JE
Tel: 07412 577 709

An earlier book of mine of Korean recipes provided the inspiration for this updated version. It has been amended to make it more accessible and interesting for readers who are new to Korean cooking.

In fact my *Easy Guide to Korean Cooking* has been something of an international project. Many dear friends, my daughter

You!

Tai and her friends, the children of my friends from many different countries and my cooking students, all came to cook with me for the photos. We were the United Nations of good food!

My sincere thanks to you all.

Yongja

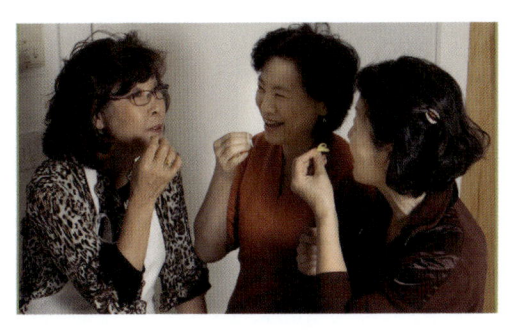

Printed in Poland
by Amazon Fulfillment
Poland Sp. z o.o., Wrocław

86342812R00084